THE BUM JOKE BOOK
fart too!

compiled by Hugh Jarse
illustrations by R. Sole

ELITE WORDS & IMAGE

WARNING: This is the only serious page in this book!

ELITE Words & Image
P O Box 24, Sherborne, Dorset, DT9 3SN

First Edition, 1992

British Library Cataloguing-in-Publication Data

A catalogue record for this book is available from the British Library.

Typesetting by ELITE Words & Image Publishing Services
Origination and Imagesetting by Regent Printers
Printed and bound in Hong Kong

ISBN 0- 9516677-4-2

FOR BUMS EVERYWHERE!

Other books in this series:

Nail on the Bannister by R. Stornaway
Lavatory Needed by Willie Makit
Constipation by Ivor Poo

Published and produced entirely by: R's Publishing Group

Published by: Smellie R's Publishing, Poo Corner, Guffyville.

Printed by: Big R's Printing Press

Page Layout and Design by Short R's Imagesetting Services

Compiled by Hugh Jarse ©
Illustrations by R Sole ©

Typeset in Poopface

Printed on Guffy Impregnated Paper

BOTTOMS UP ...

AIM ...

FIRE!!!

ODD JOBS

Little birdie flying high, dropped a message from the sky.
Oh, said the farmer, wiping his eye.
It's a jolly good thing that cows don't fly!

WHOOPSIE!

A former explorer was relating to a young woman some of his adventures.

'Once, when I was in the jungle, I was confronted by a man-eating tiger, which leapt out in front of me, and went 'R-O-A-R' !,' he said.
'Goodness, what did you do?' she enquired.
'I pooped my trousers,' he informed her.
'I think I would have done the same,' she agrees.
'No, not when the tiger leapt out, I mean , just now when I went, R-O-A-R!'

(Thanks to 'Baso')

JUST MONKEYING AROUND

Not last night, but the night before,
three little monkeys came to the door.
One had a fiddle, one had a drum,
one had a pancake stuck to his bum!

LOST PROPERTY

The doggies held a conference,
they came from near and far,
some of them came by plane
and some of them by car.

As each doggy queued,
to sign the visitors book
each doggy took its arsehole off
to hang it on a hook.

When they were assembled,
each pure bred dam and sire,
some dirty rotten bastard,
came in and shouted, FIRE.

The dogs were in a panic,
they had no time to look,
so each dog grabbed an arsehole
off the nearest hook.

And that is why you'll see today,
a dog will leave a bone,
to sniff another's arsehole,
to see if it's his own.

Can you play tennis with haemorrhoids?

No. They're too soft and they won't bounce.

ON THE JOB EMERGENCY KIT PROVIDED

A young man, taking his first lesson in lion-taming, asked the instructor what to do if the lion got off his stool and advanced,

'Take one step back and crack your whip at him,' was the reply.
'Supposing the lion still advances?'
'Keep going backwards but crack your whip more often.'
'What happens when your back's against the bars of the cage?' queried the young man.
'Reach behind you for a handful of manure and throw it in his face'.
'Supposing there isn't any manure behind me ...'
'There will be son, there will be.'

A SIGN ON A LOO WALL!

If in this bog there is no paper,
under the seat you'll find a scraper.
If the scraper cannot be found,
drag your arse along the ground.

FLUSHED WITH SUCCESS

Dan, Dan the sanitary man,
Leuitenant-General of the lavatory pan.

He puts in the paper and changes the towels,
working to the rhythm of the rumbling bowels.

ODD JOBS

Here I sit broken hearted - paid my penny and only farted.

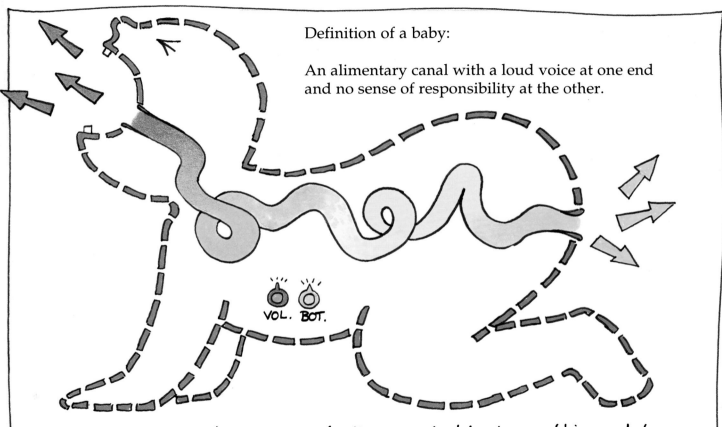

Definition of a baby:

An alimentary canal with a loud voice at one end and no sense of responsibility at the other.

VOL. BOT.

NB. Note prototype 'Volume' and 'Bottom' control knobs on this model. These are not yet available as standard, unfortunately.

THE BIRTH OF GUFFY?

A young girl went to her doctor sure that she was pregnant. The doctor told her that she wasn't, it was only wind.

A year later, the girl was pushing a pram in the High Street when the doctor saw her.

    'What have we here?' he asked, surprised.
    'A fart with a bonnet?' she replied.

Doctor, Doctor, I've got diarrhoea.

Don't worry ..... it runs in your family.

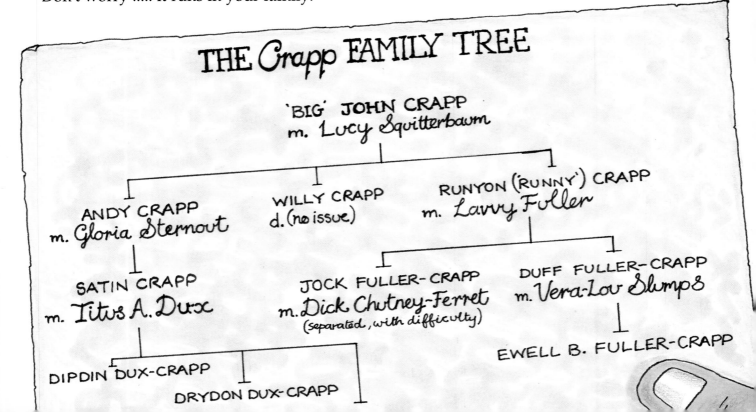

THE Crapp FAMILY TREE

'BIG' JOHN CRAPP
m. Lucy Squitterbaum

ANDY CRAPP
m. Gloria Sternout

WILLY CRAPP
d. (no issue)

RUNYON (RUNNY') CRAPP
m. Larry Fuller

SATIN CRAPP
m. Titus A. Dux

JOCK FULLER-CRAPP
m. Dick Chutney-Ferret
(separated, with difficulty)

DUFF FULLER-CRAPP
m. Vera-Lou Slumps

EWELL B. FULLER-CRAPP

DIPDIN DUX-CRAPP

DRYDON DUX-CRAPP

IGNORANCE IS BLISS

Two African gentlemen were having an in-depth conversation at a bus stop when they were joined by an old lady ...

'No, no, it's definitely W. O. O. O. M. M. B. B.,' said the first man.
'I disagree, it's W. W. W. O. O. M. B. B. B.,' said the second.

Listening intently the lady decided to put the men out of their misery and enlighten them ...

'Excuse me, but I think you'll find it's W. O. M. B., womb,' she said.
'Oh, yes,' said the first man, 'And how do you know what sound a hippopotamus makes when it farts underwater?'

(Thanks to Gary)

LADIES BEFORE GENTLEMEN? OR, IS IT AGE BEFORE BEAUTY?

Two couples were having tea around a table when one of the men inadvertantly farted.

'How dare you fart in front of my wife,' protested the other man.

'I'm sorry,' said the first, 'I didn't realise it was her turn.'

ODD JOBS

Doctor in hospital doing his rounds with the ward sister stops at the foot of a bed and looks at the patient knowingly ... ' Mmmm , rectum ...,'

'No, just missed 'em actually doctor'.

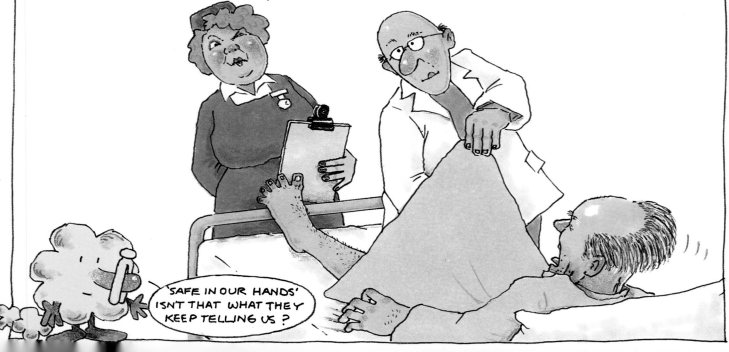

ODE TO THE GODDESS CLOSSINDA

Oh! chaste Clossinda, goddess of this place,
Shine on my efforts with propitious grace,
Soft yet consistent, let my efforts flow,
Not rudely fast nor obstinately slow.

(Thanks to Martin!)

ODD JOBS

Definition: Impossible - trying to pin diarrhoea to the wall.

FART ALERT

A sigh is but a puff of wind,
coming from the heart,
if it should take a downward course,
it's often called a fart.

To fart, it gives you pleasure,
it gives the bowels some ease,
it warms and airs the blankets,
and drives aways the fleas.

CHEEKY PROBLEM

If skirts become much shorter, said the typist with a blush,
there'll be two more cheeks to powder,
and a lot more hair to brush!

ODD JOBS

Definition: A bum - Kojak with a parting.

Knock, knock.   Who's there ?   ***ODD JOBS***

Nicholas.   Nicholas who?

Nicholas girls shouldn't climb ladders.

ROCKET MAN

There was a young man from Great Horton.
Who had a peculiar short'un.
But to make up for this loss,
He had balls like a hoss,
And a fart like a 650 Norton.

GUFFY OPERA!

A man goes to a theatrical agents, claiming that he can speak clearly through his back passage ...

'I just have to see this,' says the agent, 'show me.'

The man stands up and lets rip ...

'You can't call that talking,' exclaims the agent!

'I haven't started yet,' comes the reply, 'I was just clearing my throat!'

(Thanks to 'Baso' ... again!)

NECESSITY IS THE MASTER OF INVENTION!

With unemployment figures high and interviews, let alone jobs, hard to come by, Willy the wally is desperate for a job to support his old mum. Willy does finally receive a letter asking him to attend an interview, and Willy is rewarded with a trial period during which he must prove his skills as a toothbrush salesman.

The first week goes by without any sales. Willy is told that he really must pull his socks up if he wants to keep the job. The second week sees a slight improvement, but not enough he's told. The third week arrives and his prospects are looking very poor, but seeing Willy's unhappy, but eager face his boss decides to give him a tip.

> 'You need to get yourself a gimmick - you'll sell hundreds then and you'll be able to keep the job!'

The following week Willy returns to the office with astounding sales figures and is rewarded with a permanent job. However, intrigued by the sudden results achieved by Willy, his boss tracks him to the local shopping centre where he finds that Willy has set up a stall giving away cakes! He just can't see the connection so he creeps a bit nearer to hear what's being said:

Man - angrily: 'These cakes taste like shit!'
Wally: 'Tis shit wanna buy a toothbrush?'

(Thanks to Graham!)

ODD JOBS

What's the difference between the moon and the River Severn.

The moon is shiny bright ...

ODD JOBS

What's the last thing that goes through a bug's mind when it hits your windscreen?

Its arse.

NO TISSUE REQUIRED

A couple were admiring the view at the seaside, when a seagull
flew overhead and dropped a 'blessing' on the lady's head.

'Don't just stand there,' she says to her husband,
'Get a tissue or something.'
'What's the use?' he replies, 'It'll be miles away by now.'

IT'S A BUMMER

Trailing at the end of a flock of geese, all possessing yellow beaks,
was a goose with a brown beak.

A bird from another flock asked,

'Hey, why have all your mates got yellow beaks and you've got a brown one?'
'Well,' he replied, ' I can fly as fast as they can; but I can't stop as quick.'

Enquiry to Export Company about possible markets - sent on April 1st!

Midlands beef farmer has copious supplies of selected animal manure suitable for export market.

Supplies can be despatched in bulk loads by articulated trailer, or packaged in handy 50 kg sacks suitable for the larger garden. Small handy-packs are supplied shrink wrapped in household sized sachets which are ideal for rejuvenating spent gro-bags, or invigorating window box soils.

The manure is high in phosphates and newly discovered poly-unsaturated phosphates, which are believed to increase crop yields by a factor of four.

Farmer Jim is looking to identify opportunities to trade with European growers and horticulturists and believes that, once it catches on, Super - X - Crement will gradually spread all over the community.

The secret of the potent bi-product, says the farmer, lies in the little known fact that manure from the male animal is of a higher quality than that from the female.

And that makes this a load of bull-shit - Mmmmoooo.

(Thanks to Wyn!)

THE END